I0505560

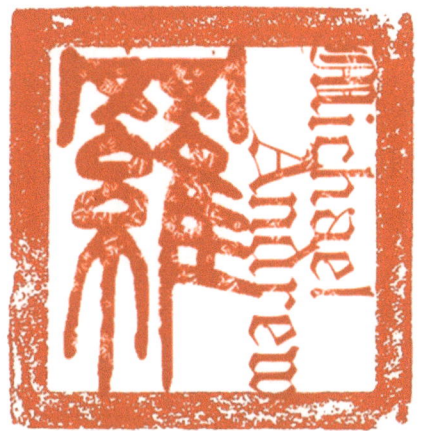

© Law Cheuk Yui / Michael Andrew Law. All Rights Reserved.

Copyright © 2015 by Law Cheuk Yui

All rights reserved.

Cover design by Law Cheuk Yui / cheukyui.com
Book design by Law Cheuk Yui

No part of this book may be reproduced in any form or by any
electronic or mechanical means including information storage
and retrieval systems, without permission in writing from the
author. The only exception is by a reviewer, who may quote
short excerpts in a review.

This book may include works of fiction. Names, characters,
places, and incidents either are products of the author's
imagination or are used fictitiously. Any resemblance to
actual persons, living or dead, events, or locales is entirely
coincidental.

Michael Andrew Law
Visit my website at www.michaelandrewlaw.com

First Printing: 2015
Shop Cheuk Yui

Michael Andrew Law

(852) 6444-7550
info@michaelandrewlaw.com
www.michaelandrewlaw.com

The Pale Hair : Conceptz

Medium : Traditional Oil Painting (With Acrylic Based) , Glitter , Gold Leaf .
About This Serie : Created after the third Series of painting of The
Pale Hair Girls Original Series Paintings , Done with mixed media on Wood
or /andcanvas ,an more experiential works by Michael Andrew Law , explores
a more Painterliness style , also express his love to Fashion illustration.
Number of Paintings : 30 (As of 2015)
Availability : Limited Edition , Prints , Original Painting

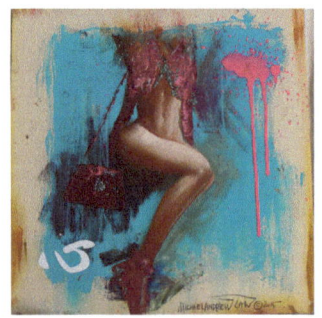
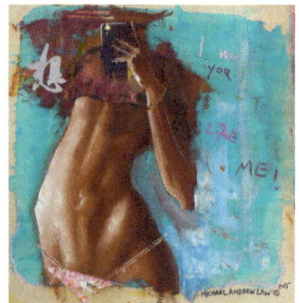
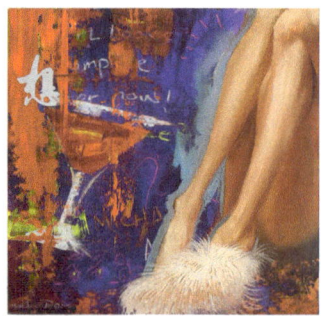

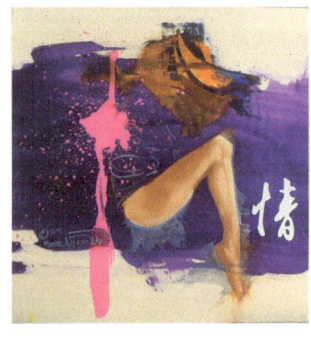
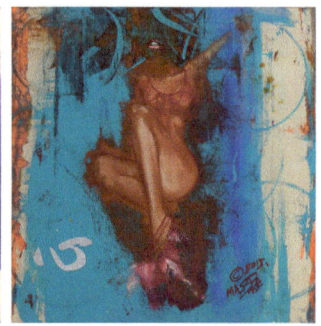
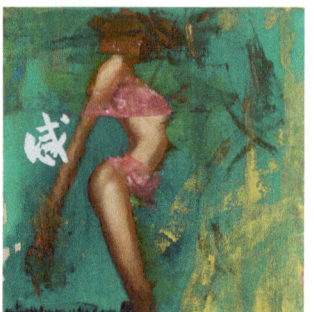

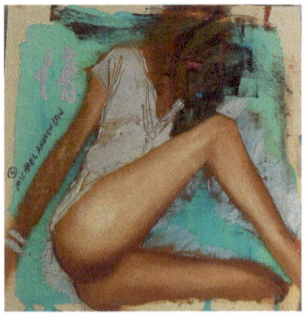
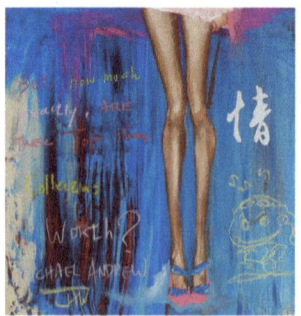
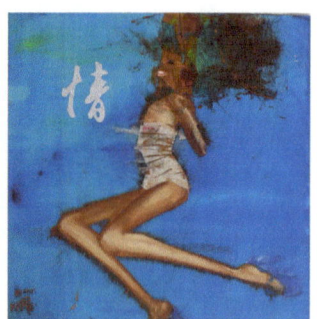

關 於藝術家MICHAEL ANDREW LAW:

生長於交接時期香港的年輕藝術家 Michael Andrew Law，擅長把數碼繪圖，Pop 摩登藝術及古典油畫揉合時事及諷刺，創出獨特的視覺藝術語言及內容，跨越中西混合背景思維界限，探索互聯網世代交錯回歸的中西混雜之香港歷史。

他以自由隨意的手法結合摩登及古典材料與技巧，保持表現與認知、控制與隨性、魯妄與機智、自我與社羣等對立美學力量之間的張力，並對香港Y世代、本土文化及民族社會的殘酷現實作出尖刻的評論。Michael Andrew Law 的作品色彩豐富，寫實風格描繪的冰山美人，刻畫在滿佈流行文化圖像、東方書法標誌及符號的背景上。《白髮女孩系列》(The Pale Hair Girls，2006 — 2013 年) 的創作之中，Michael Andrew Law 獨特的繪畫風格呈獻出達達主義思考方式般的且出人意表的效果。畫中冰山美人式的人物穿插在抽象的香港和俗世符號上。

Pale Hair Girls系列的畫作的視覺靈感大量源自法國美術學院派大師William-Adolphe Bouguereau 的少年油畫作品以及已故華裔畫家陳逸飛的史詩及美人作品，Michael Andrew Law一反傳統的繪畫技法，以數碼混合古典繪畫技，重新演繹細緻複雜的中西方古典畫面和精心網絡細思考的構圖，以西式媒介呼應中國的傳統書法裡作為圖案之筆觸，在Michael Andrew Law的筆下這種交錯西式POP ART和中式古典藝術表現時輪廓卻非常細緻，尤其最廣為流傳和臨摹的Leonardo da Vinci作品Mona Lisa (1517 年)，以東方血統之妻子肖像取代Mona Lisa 的表徵意義，極具質感的厚顏料同時呈現寫生畫作時人物肉體的細微變化。

《誰會理會不是自已的新天地:三聯畫》（Humanity）刻畫了在世代末日的未來世代們於本為廢墟的香港島上，等待著他們的命運。這些離奇的場景與Jerry B. Jenkins及Timothy LaHaye等當代作家描寫的超現實、宗教解讀、未來主義情懷如出一致。於半島酒店扶輪會演講當代藝術

主要探索他藝術裡其中一項最重要的二分法：浪漫與嘲諷、作為藝術家對美的浪漫思考及交滙中西混合背景思維之香港Y世代的悲情，由天真燦爛的冰山美人式少女與可怕的末日和俗物之間的強烈對比作像徵。無論是標誌性的單幅「古典書法圖案的無身份肖像」，抑或以三聯畫形式出現，運用到大師級繪畫與構圖技巧，揉合了精細傳統油畫技法與摩登畫的表現方式建構，美人亦在美術史和流行文化裡是永恆的主題。冰山美人式少女令人聯想到生命的脆弱與時光飛逝之無情。藝術家就是要了解不同世界之間的界線並翻譯到不同文化價值之間的語境如高尚對低俗、古代對現代、東方對西方。

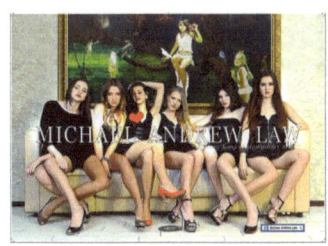

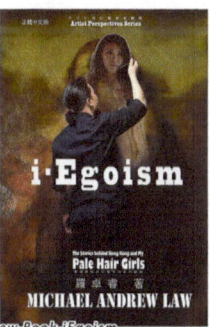

New Book iEgoism
ISBN:978-1-4990-2124-0

憑著 iEgoism 故事性的風格和精神，Michael Andrew Law將流行、古典與時事內容混合成一種感覺超豐富的視覺藝術作品，所涉獵的美學領域和文化靈感不斷延伸，而他在當中游走自如。一如常見的當代藝術主題，去作為「諷刺」及「反思」有關「浪漫」與「悲情」的直接敘述。

他所開發的iEgoism主題，就深受當代或反傳統藝術愛好者的喜愛，這被視為跟西方DADA藝術主義互相呼應。Michael Andrew Law把自己置身於他熱烈的自我網世代主義- iEgoism裡展現出的姿態卻是完全屬於他本人和他的時代的。

Michael Andrew Law於2006 年隨美國紐約藝術家Daniel Anderson深造古典油畫，其後發展純美術繪畫工作，2008年獲贊助於香港中環成立藝術工作室 Nature Art。除了製作藝術及相關作品，Nature Art 及 Michael Andrew Law 亦積極培育香港年輕藝術家。

2013 年，他於NatureArt Gallery舉行藝術展覽《iEgoism》，從香港歷史中追溯當代香港流行視覺藝術文化的特徵。

Michael Andrew Law 的作品曾於紐約 Chelsea 的聯合展覽中展出，他亦曾在著名機構及學校舉行個展及講座，例如星光大道 (2009 年)、天主教香港教區、香港中央圖書館(2004 -2007 年)、灣仔政府大樓外(2004 年)、香港會議展覽中心 (2003 年)。2015出版藝術文字著作《不可不知的藝術家觀點系列-iEgoism》更深入探討香港Y世代、香港歷史和Michael Andrew Law的作品脈絡關聯。

Michael Andrew Law 現於香港定居及從事創作。

Painting by Michael Andrew Law
©2015 Law Cheuk Yui. All rights reserved

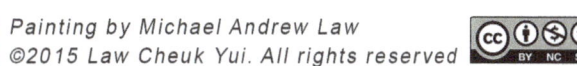

Michael Andrew Law fusing digital and classical painting with west and East creative philosophy , to produce an extremely original artistic language and content that bridged west and east ,classical and modern medium , at the same time clearly tells the stories of his own generation. Combining digital creative materials and classical painting techniques with effusive yet knowing and precise focused , his paintings maintain a powerful tension between opposing aesthetic forces—expression and knowledge, control and spontaneity, savagery and wit, urbanity and primitivism—while providing satiric commentary on the oppressive realities of the predicament of Generation Internet, homegrown hongkonger's local-culture vesus Traditional Chinese culture, and The Hong Kong's post-handover history.

In his dynamically designed compositions, gracefully detailed figures and innocent faces are incise against fields that juxtaposed with portraits, chinese calligraphy, and sometimes cgi. The Pale Hair Girls Series (2006 - 2013) depicts realistic cold, icy-like young female figures surrounded by abstract and expressively painted forms and shapes revealing images of Pop culture, Historial figures, and Hong Kong landmarks.

Michael Andrew Law draws inspiration from Old Master's works such as Caravaggio , Ruben , Rembrandt , all the way to the Modern Art Superstars such as Warhol , Lichtenstein , Richter , De Kooning , Bacon , Wool and Prince . The Pale Hair Girls series mainly inspired by the painting works of French academic painter and traditionalist William-Adolphe Bouguereau and the Late Great YiFei Chen's characteristic "Romantic Realism" paintings.

In a reversal of standard East-West aesthetics, Law re-interprets Old Master's sophisticated imagery combine classical and digital materials—which resonate with Digital Vector Designs and Paintings—with fine strokes of oil paint multi-layered with paint film.In his interpretation of Leonardo Da Vinci's iconic Mona Lisa's smile (1517)—an iconic image that has been endlessly disseminated and reproduced—Law painted over the symbolism of the portrait Mona Lisa with his young wife , intent on rendering the figure in contemporary fashion with the iconic image as background .

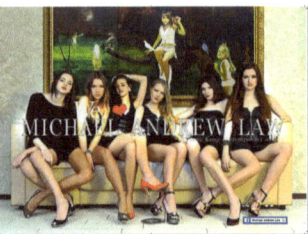
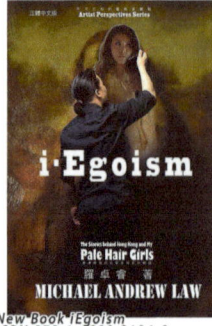

New Book iEgoism
ISBN:978-1-4990-2124-0

"The Humanity triptych" depicts New Generation HongKongers in a Ruined Hong Kong city , awaiting their unknown fate of a new beginning. This painting series explores one of the central paradox of his art—between romance and derision , his romantic magnanimity as an artist and his pessimistic perspective on the predicament of Generation Y Hongkongers. Here, this paradox is symbolized by the stark contrast of icy cold young female and disturbing representations of the armageddon-like of images. Whether portrayed as single "chinese calligraphy " or in triptych composition and classical paintwork that combine both expressive and traditional painting techniques with the digital vector , the beauties and the human figures stand as eternal motifs in the history of art and also in popular culture. Both oppositional and parallel, they are reminders of the fragile vibrancy of life and the impitoyable passing of time.

A references between different cultural refrence (high/pop, classical/contemporary, east/west), Michael Andrew Law has stated that an artist should be someone who understood how to hybrid between different worlds and go ahead makes an effort to knowing them. With his distinctive "iEgoism" philosophy , which employs highly refined academic painting techniques to depict a mixture of abstract expressionism within a representational pop culture images. These techniques parallel to the themes of romance and predicament of this generation , he recollects and revitalizes narratives of irony and introspection.

Michael Andrew Lawwas born in 1982 in British Hong Kong , studied fine art with american artist Daniel Anderson and graduate of China Central Academy of Fine Arts Sam Zeng from 2003 - 2006 . He co-founded the Hong Kong Art Studio Nature Art Workshop in 2008. In addition to the production and marketing of Michael Andrew Law's art and related work, Nature Art functions as a supportive environment for the fostering of emerging Hong Konger artists. Law is also a curator. In 2013, he organized an exhibition of contemporary art titled "iEgoism ," which served as a narration of contemporary HongKong Gen Y pop culture .

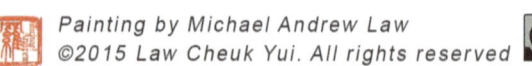
Painting by Michael Andrew Law
©2015 Law Cheuk Yui. All rights reserved
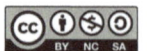

Michael Andrew Law

(852) 6444-7550

info@michaelandrewlaw.com
www.michaelandrewlaw.com

Selected publications

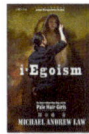

iEgoism by Michael Andrew Law
Softcover : 110 pages
Publisher : Xlibris LLC
ISBN: Softcover 978-1-4990-2124-0
ISBN: EBook 978-1-4990-2118-9

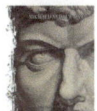

Michael Andrew Law The early years volume one: Nine Drawings from the early years collection
ISBN-10: 1503319407
ISBN-13: 978-1503319400

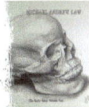

Michael Andrew Law The early years volume Two: Nine more Drawings from the early years collection (Volume 2)
ISBN-10: 1503365085
ISBN-13: 978-1503365087

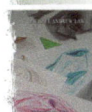

Michael Andrew Law The early years volume Three: Nine Drawings from the early years collection (Volume 3)
ISBN-10: 1503366065
ISBN-13: 978-1503366060
Product Dimensions: 6 x 0.1 x 9 inches

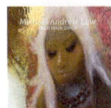

Michael Andrew Law: Pale Hair Girls Catalogue (Volume 1)
Paperback: 124 pages
ISBN-10: 1503372111
ISBN-13: 978-1503372115
Product Dimensions: 8.5 x 0.3 x 8.5 inches

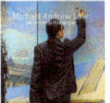

December To Remember: Michael Andrew Law Exhibition
Paperback: 120 pages
ISBN-10: 1505609259
ISBN-13: 978-1505609257

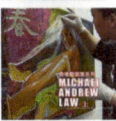

Hong Kong Artist Series: Michael Andrew Law 1
Paperback: 48 pages
ISBN-10: 1507580665
ISBN-13: 978-1507580660

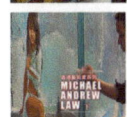

Hong Kong Artist Series: Michael Andrew Law 2'
Paperback: 48 pages
ISBN-10: 1507581556
ISBN-13: 978-1507581551

Painting by Michael Andrew Law
©2015 Law Cheuk Yui. All rights reserved

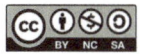

Michael Andrew Law

(852) 6444-7550
info@michaelandrewlaw.com
www.michaelandrewlaw.com

Publications : Illustrated Books

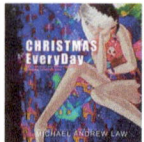

Christmas Everyday Book 1: Pale Hair Girls Christmas Series (Pale Hair Girls Christmas Everyday) (Volume 1)
ISBN-10: 1505453216
ISBN-13: 978-1505453218
Product Dimensions: 8.5 x 0.1 x 8.5 inches

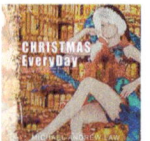

Christmas Everyday Book 2: Pale Hair Girls Christmas Series (Pale Hair Girls Christmas Everyday) (Volume 2)
ISBN-10: 1505467799
ISBN-13: 978-1505467796
Product Dimensions: 8.5 x 0.1 x 8.5 inches

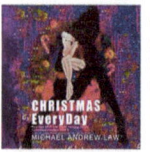
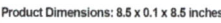

Christmas Everyday Book 3: Pale Hair Girls Christmas Series (Pale Hair Girls Christmas Everyday) (Volume 3)
ISBN-10: 1505468051
ISBN-13: 978-1505468052
Product Dimensions: 8.5 x 0.1 x 8.5 inches

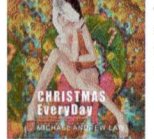
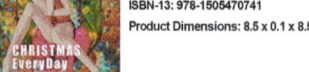

Christmas Everyday Book 4: Pale Hair Girls Christmas Series (Pale Hair Girls Christmas Everyday) (Volume 4)
ISBN-10: 1505470749
ISBN-13: 978-1505470741
Product Dimensions: 8.5 x 0.1 x 8.5 inches

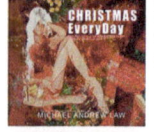

Christmas Everyday Book 5: Pale Hair Girls Christmas Series (Pale Hair Girls Christmas Everyday) (Volume 5)
ISBN-10: 1505470854
ISBN-13: 978-1505470857
Product Dimensions: 8.5 x 0.1 x 8.5 inches

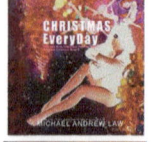

Christmas Everyday Book 6: Pale Hair Girls Christmas Series (Pale Hair Girls Christmas Everyday) (Volume 6)
ISBN-10: 150547115X
ISBN-13: 978-1505471151
Product Dimensions: 8.5 x 0.1 x 8.5 inches

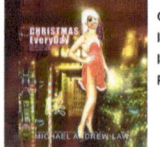

Christmas Everyday: Special Edition (Pale Hair Girls Christmas Everyday) (Volume 7)
ISBN-10: 1505583926
ISBN-13: 978-1505583922
Product Dimensions: 8.5 x 0.3 x 8.5 inches

Painting by Michael Andrew Law
©2015 Law Cheuk Yui. All rights reserved
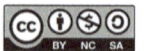

Michael Andrew Law

(852) 6444-7550
info@michaelandrewlaw.com
www.michaelandrewlaw.com

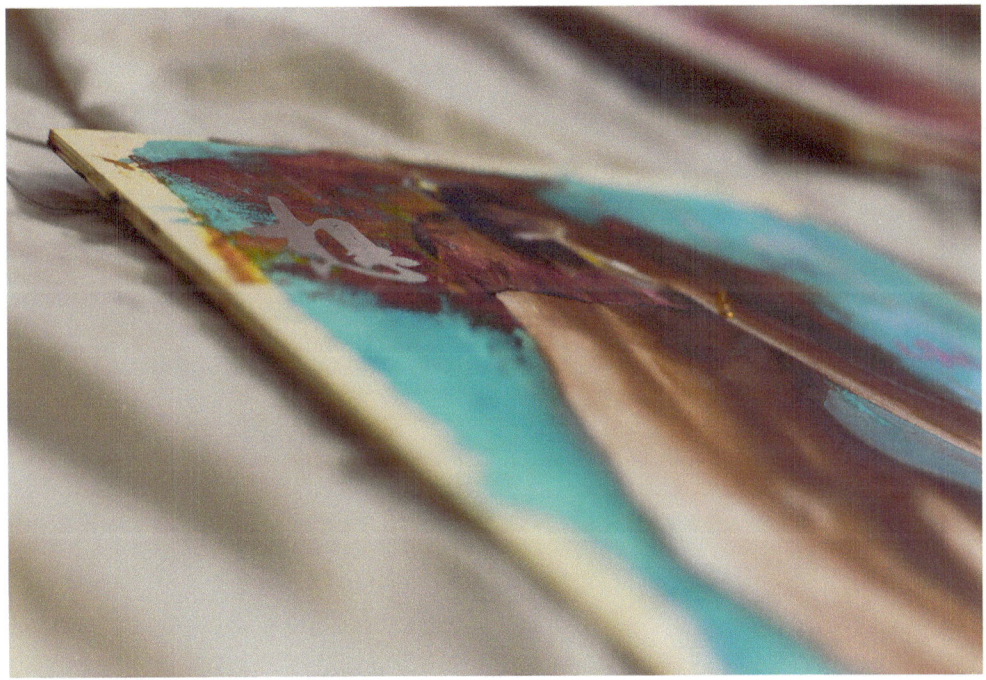

DETAILS of a painting
Oil , Glitter and Gold leaf on wood
12 x 12 inches
Private Collection

Michael Andrew Law

(852) 6444-7550
info@michaelandrewlaw.com
www.michaelandrewlaw.com

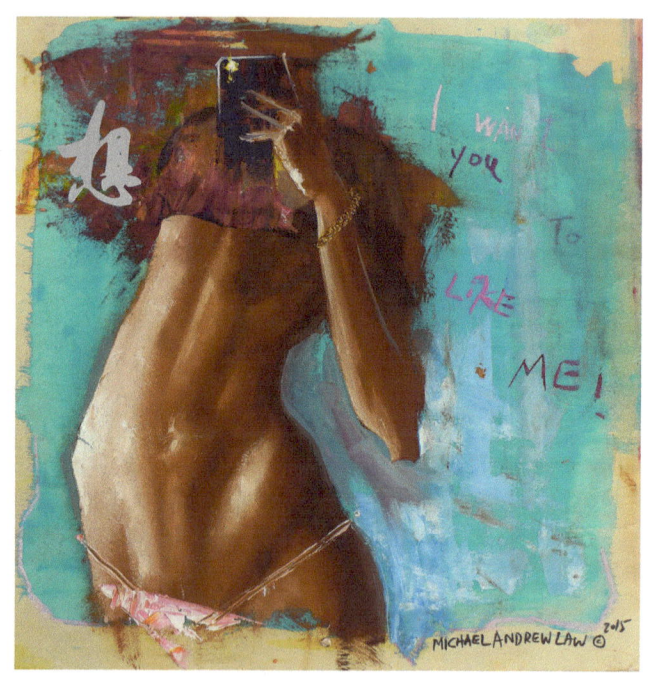

Oil , Glitter and Gold leaf on wood

12 x 12 inches

Private Collection

Michael Andrew Law

(852) 6444-7550
info@michaelandrewlaw.com
www.michaelandrewlaw.com

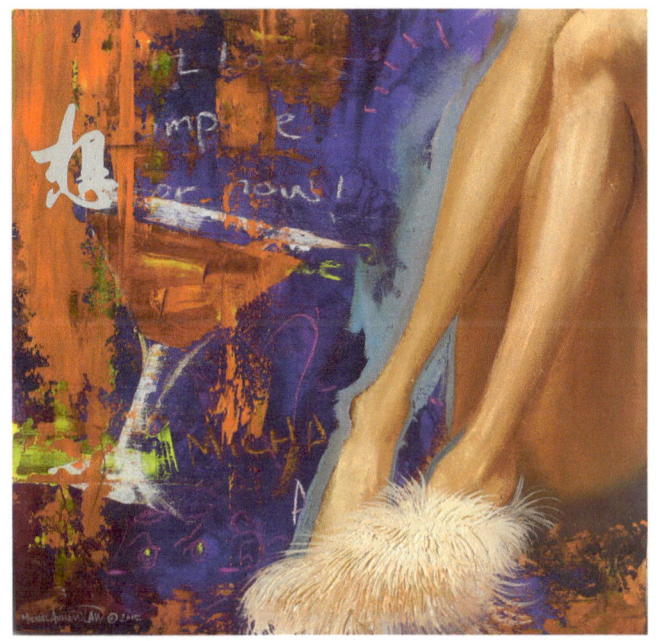

Oil , Glitter and Gold leaf on wood

12 x 12 inches

Private Collection

Michael Andrew Law

(852) 6444-7550

info@michaelandrewlaw.com

www.michaelandrewlaw.com

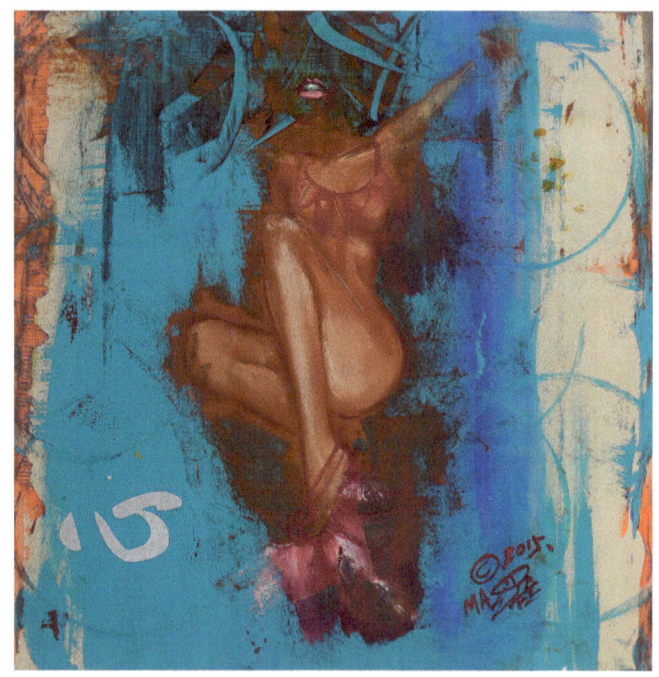

Oil , Glitter and Gold leaf on wood

12 x 12 inches

Private Collection

Michael Andrew Law

(852) 6444-7550
info@michaelandrewlaw.com
www.michaelandrewlaw.com

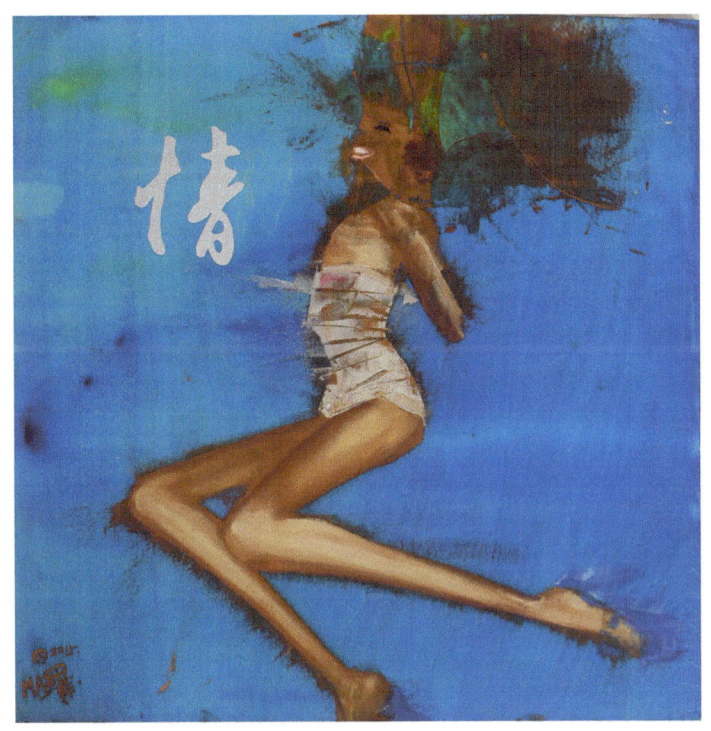

Oil , Glitter and Gold leaf on wood

12 x 12 inches

Private Collection

Michael Andrew Law

(852) 6444-7550
info@michaelandrewlaw.com
www.michaelandrewlaw.com

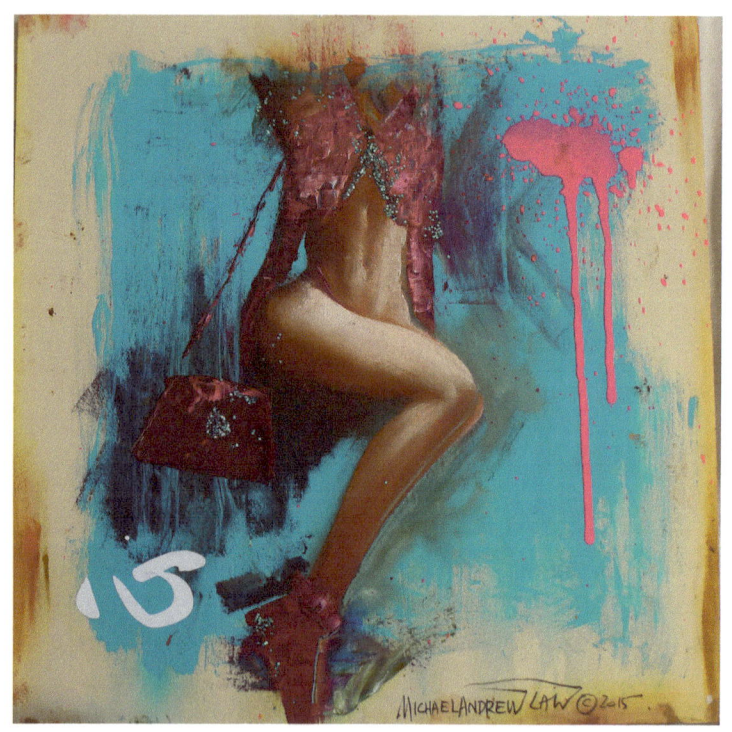

Oil , Glitter and Gold leaf on wood

12 x 12 inches

Private Collection

Michael Andrew Law

(852) 6444-7550

info@michaelandrewlaw.com

www.michaelandrewlaw.com

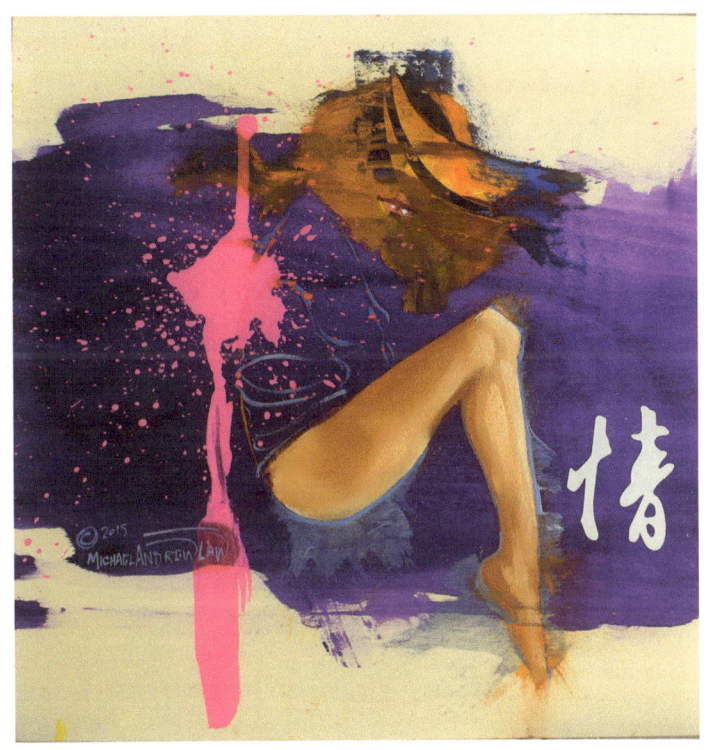

Oil , Glitter and Gold leaf on wood

12 x 12 inches

Private Collection

Michael Andrew Law

(852) 6444-7550

info@michaelandrewlaw.com

www.michaelandrewlaw.com

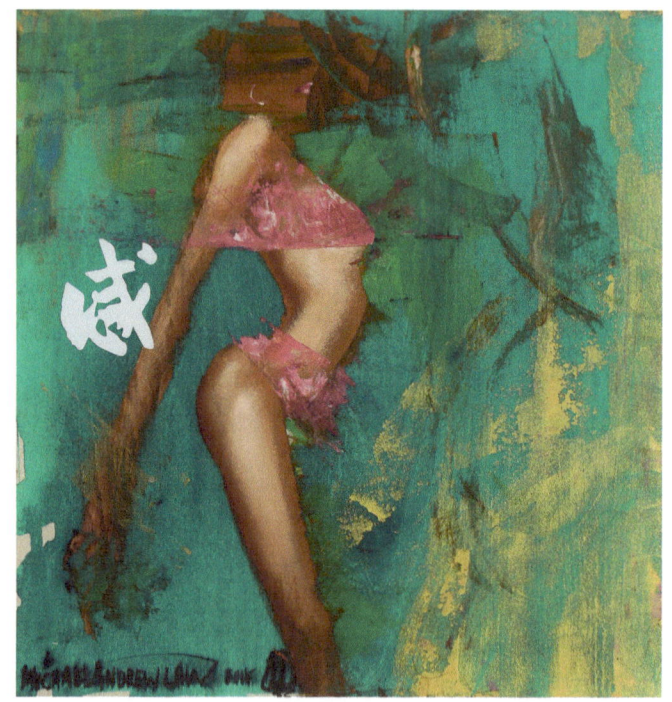

Oil , Glitter and Gold leaf on wood

12 x 12 inches

Private Collection

Michael Andrew Law

(852) 6444-7550

info@michaelandrewlaw.com

www.michaelandrewlaw.com

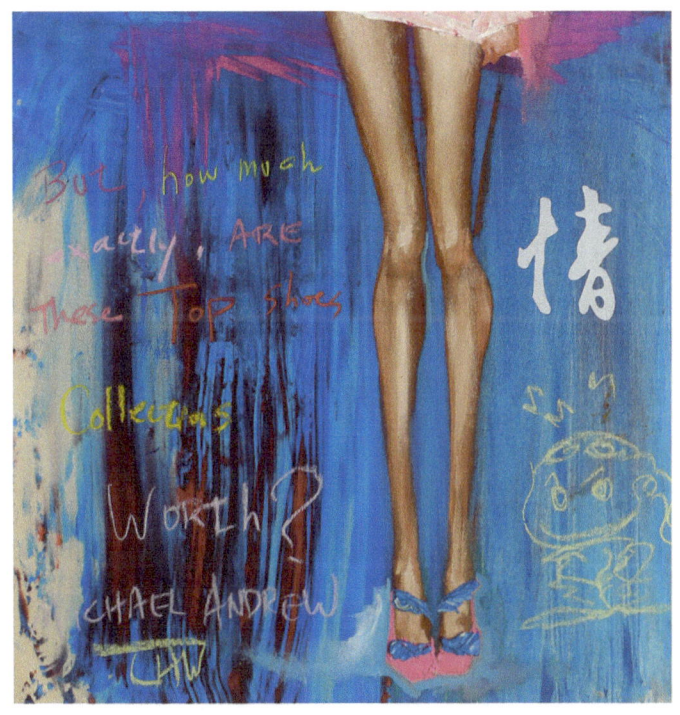

Oil , Glitter and Gold leaf on wood

12 x 12 inches

Private Collection

Michael Andrew Law
(852) 6444-7550
info@michaelandrewlaw.com
www.michaelandrewlaw.com

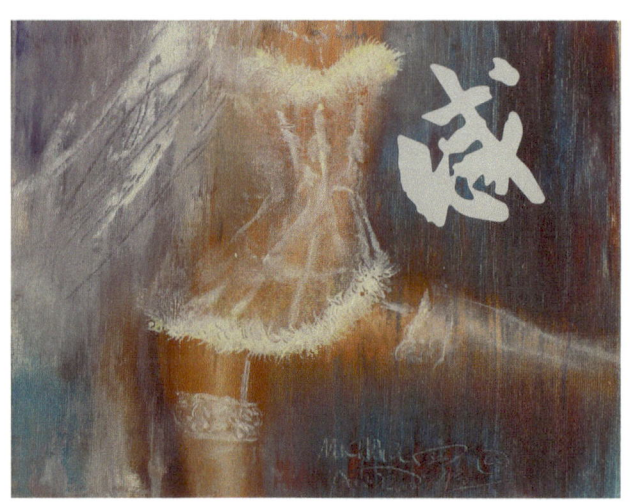

DETAILS of a painting

Oil , Glitter and Gold leaf on wood

12 x 12 inches

Private Collection

Michael Andrew Law

(852) 6444-7550
info@michaelandrewlaw.com
www.michaelandrewlaw.com

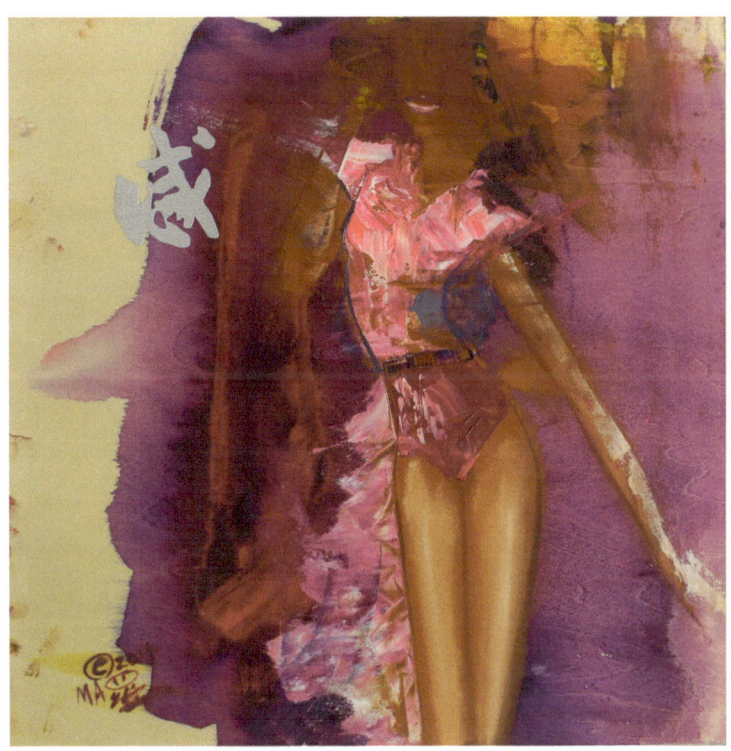

DETAILS of a painting

Oil , Glitter and Gold leaf on wood

12 x 12 inches

Private Collection

Michael Andrew Law

(852) 6444-7550

info@michaelandrewlaw.com

www.michaelandrewlaw.com

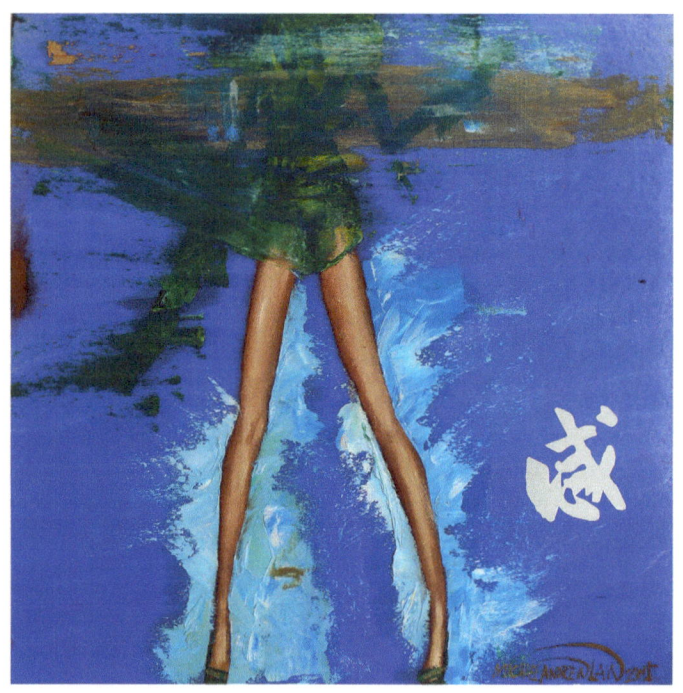

Oil , Glitter and Gold leaf on wood

12 x 12 inches

Private Collection

Michael Andrew Law

(852) 6444-7550
info@michaelandrewlaw.com
www.michaelandrewlaw.com

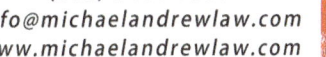

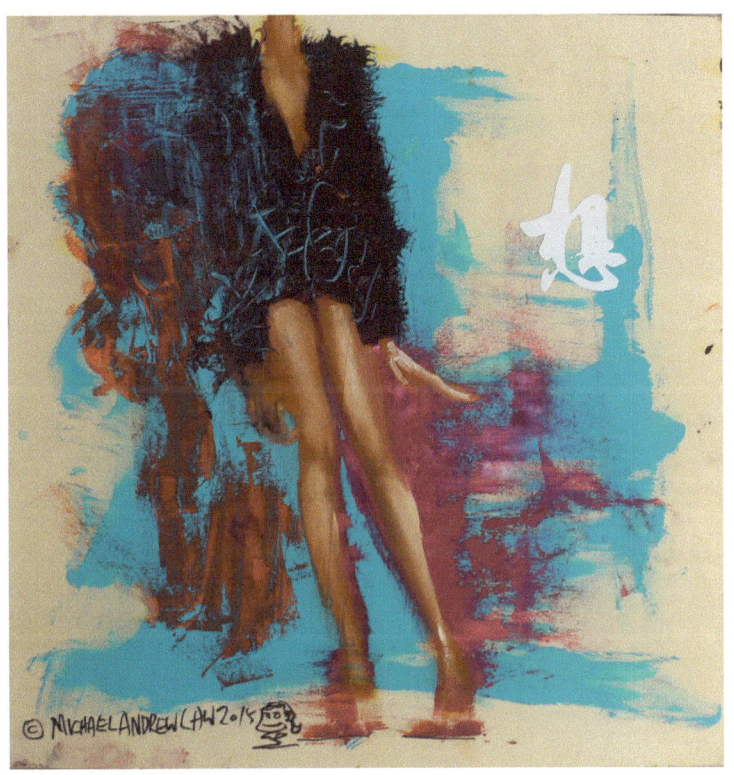

Oil , Glitter and Gold leaf on wood

12 x 12 inches

Private Collection

Michael Andrew Law

(852) 6444-7550
info@michaelandrewlaw.com
www.michaelandrewlaw.com

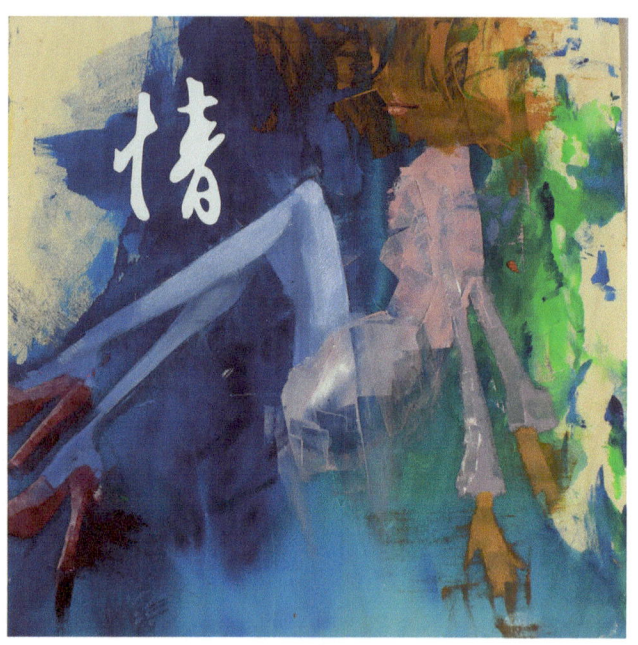

Oil , Glitter and Gold leaf on wood

12 x 12 inches

Private Collection

Michael Andrew Law

(852) 6444-7550

info@michaelandrewlaw.com

www.michaelandrewlaw.com

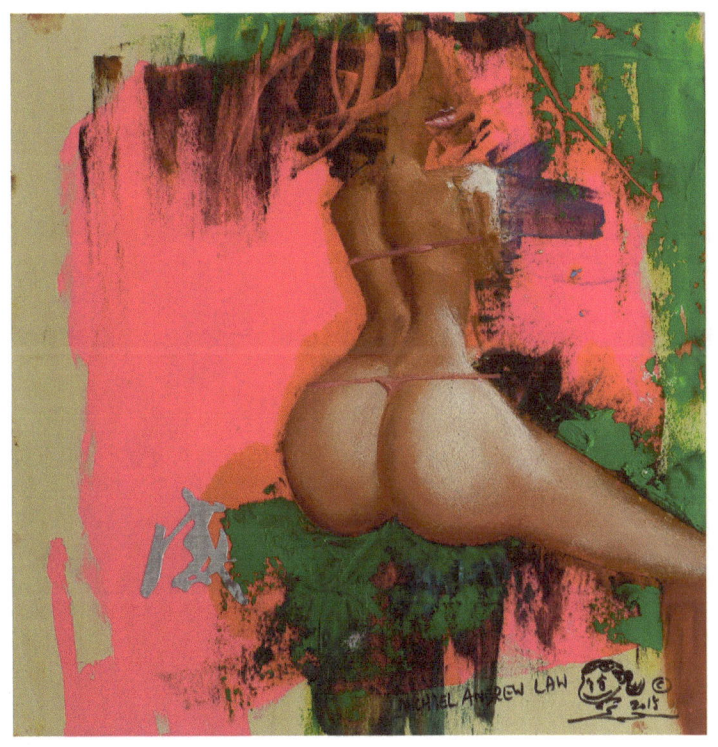

Oil , Glitter and Gold leaf on wood

12 x 12 inches

Private Collection

Michael Andrew Law

(852) 6444-7550

info@michaelandrewlaw.com

www.michaelandrewlaw.com

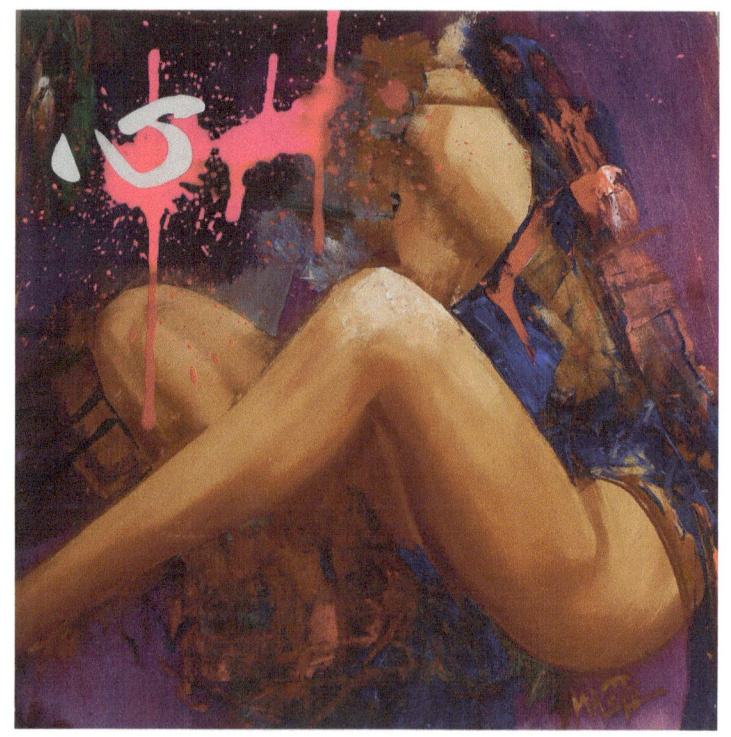

Oil , Glitter and Gold leaf on wood

12 x 12 inches

Private Collection

Michael Andrew Law

(852) 6444-7550
info@michaelandrewlaw.com
www.michaelandrewlaw.com

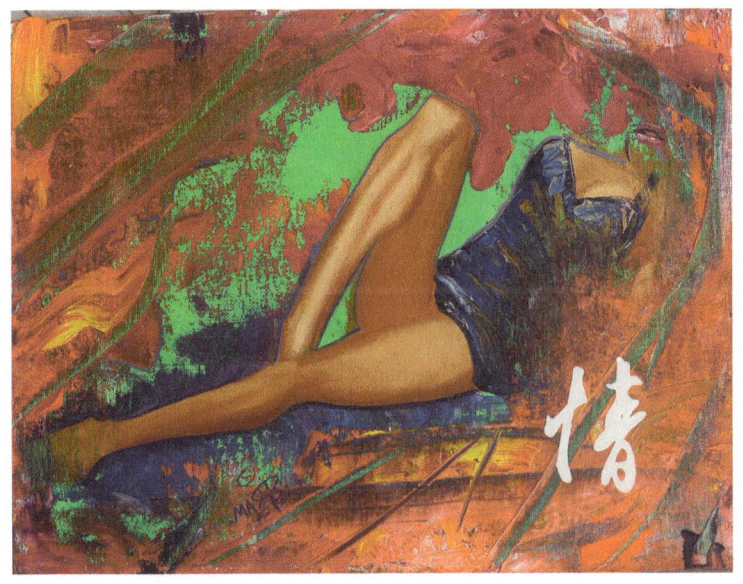

Oil , Glitter and Gold leaf on wood

12 x 12 inches

Private Collection

Michael Andrew Law

(852) 6444-7550

info@michaelandrewlaw.com

www.michaelandrewlaw.com

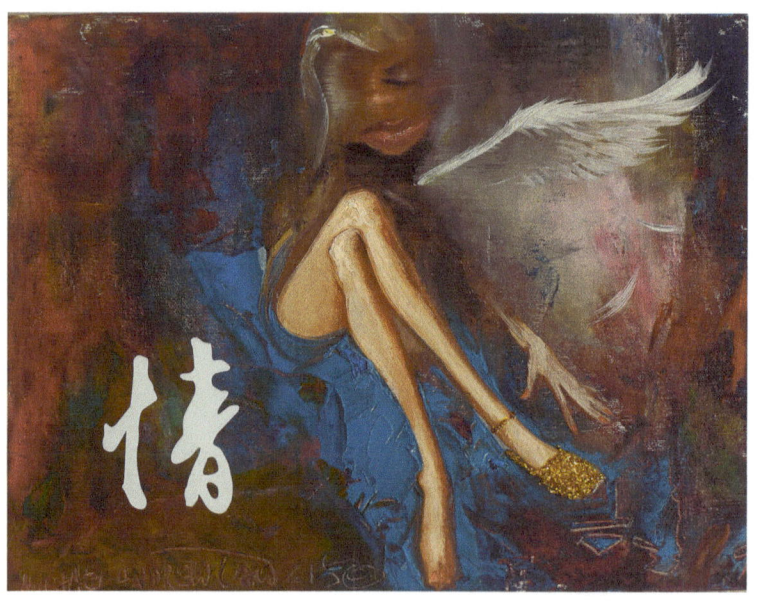

Oil , Glitter and Gold leaf on wood

12 x 12 inches

Private Collection

Michael Andrew Law

(852) 6444-7550

info@michaelandrewlaw.com

www.michaelandrewlaw.com

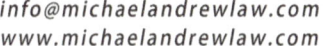

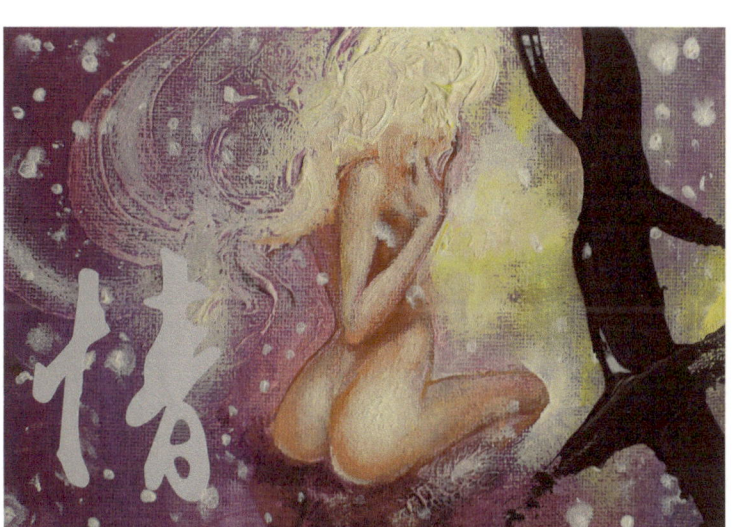

Oil , Glitter and Gold leaf on wood

12 x 12 inches

Private Collection

Michael Andrew Law

(852) 6444-7550

info@michaelandrewlaw.com
www.michaelandrewlaw.com

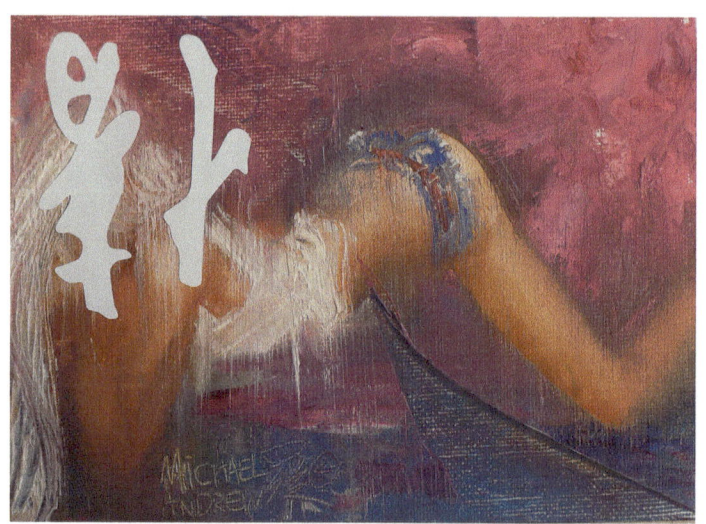

Oil , Glitter and Gold leaf on wood

12 x 12 inches

Private Collection

Michael Andrew Law

(852) 6444-7550
info@michaelandrewlaw.com
www.michaelandrewlaw.com

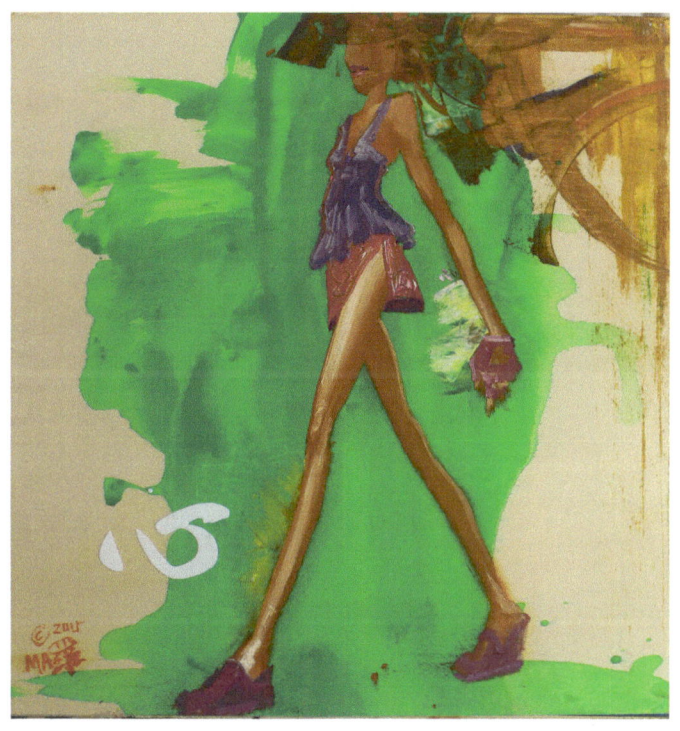

Oil , Glitter and Gold leaf on wood

12 x 12 inches

Private Collection

Michael Andrew Law

(852) 6444-7550
info@michaelandrewlaw.com
www.michaelandrewlaw.com

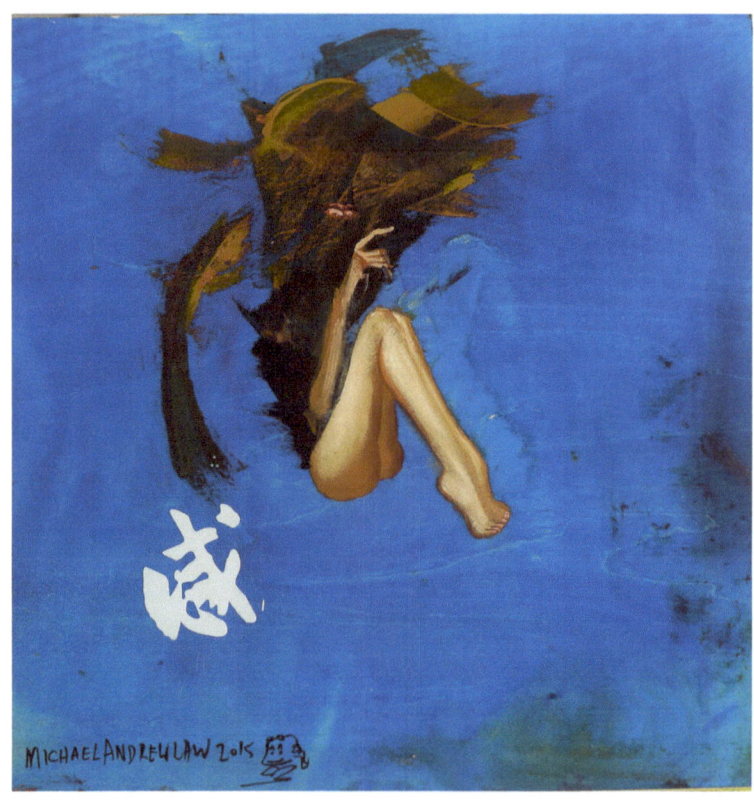

Oil , Glitter and Gold leaf on wood

12 x 12 inches

Private Collection

Michael Andrew Law

(852) 6444-7550
info@michaelandrewlaw.com
www.michaelandrewlaw.com

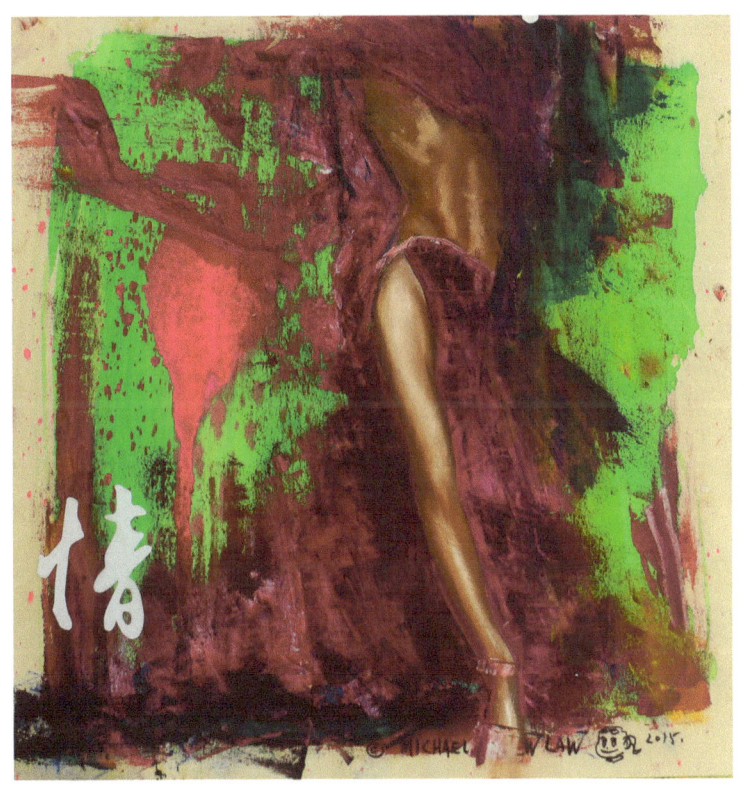

Oil , Glitter and Gold leaf on wood

12 x 12 inches

Private Collection

Michael Andrew Law

(852) 6444-7550

info@michaelandrewlaw.com

www.michaelandrewlaw.com

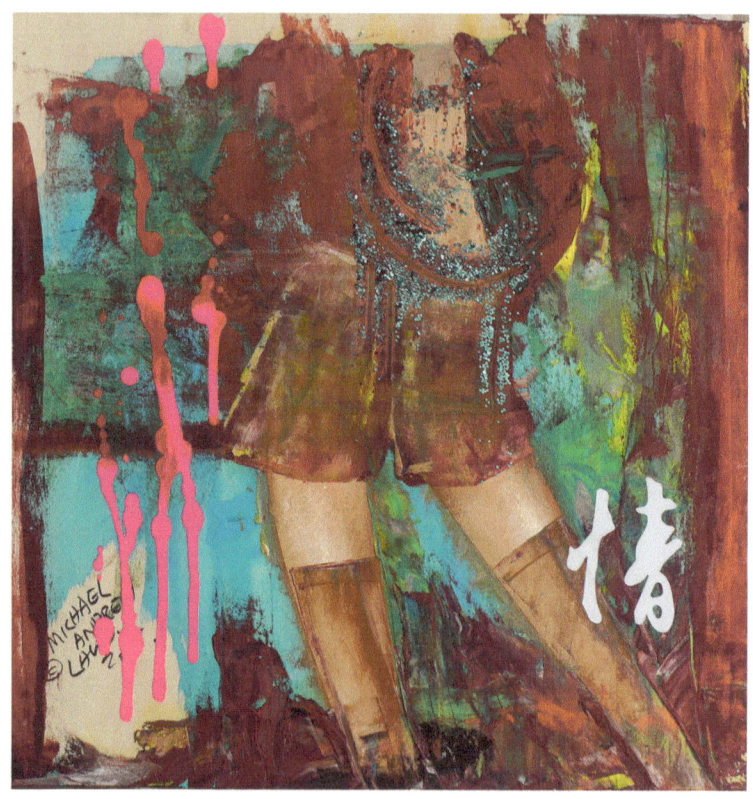

Oil , Glitter and Gold leaf on wood

12 x 12 inches

Private Collection

Michael Andrew Law

(852) 6444-7550
info@michaelandrewlaw.com
www.michaelandrewlaw.com

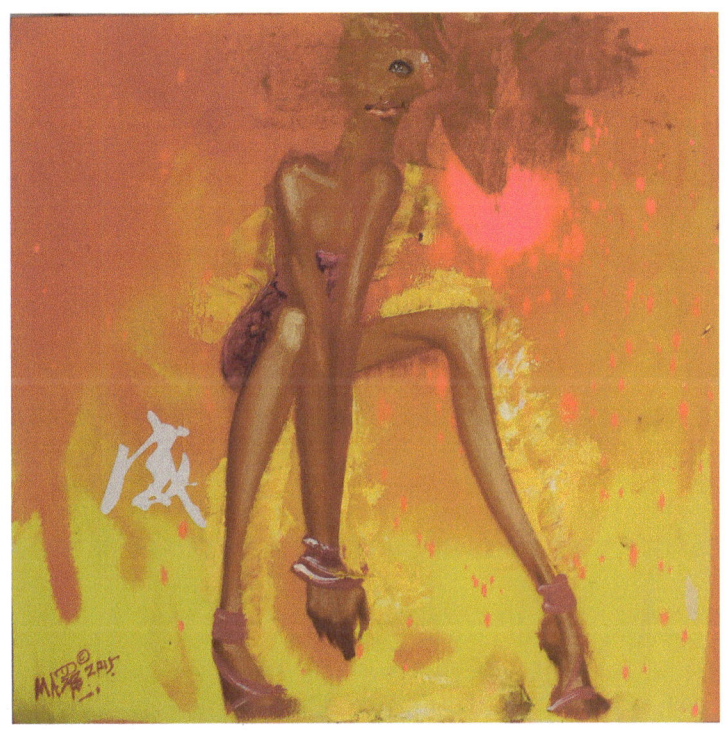

Oil , Glitter and Gold leaf on wood

12 x 12 inches

Private Collection

Michael Andrew Law

(852) 6444-7550

info@michaelandrewlaw.com

www.michaelandrewlaw.com

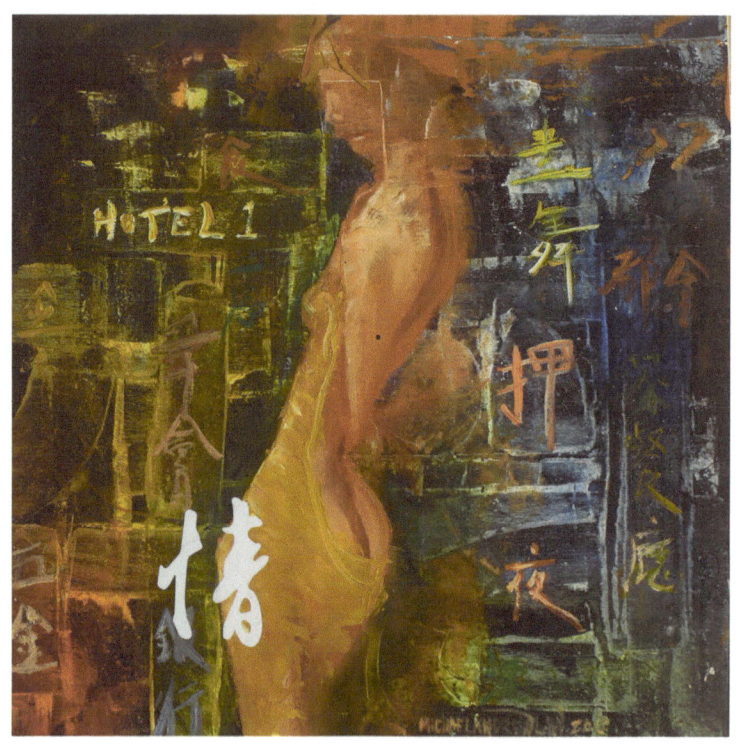

Oil , Glitter and Gold leaf on wood

12 x 12 inches

Private Collection

Michael Andrew Law

(852) 6444-7550
info@michaelandrewlaw.com
www.michaelandrewlaw.com

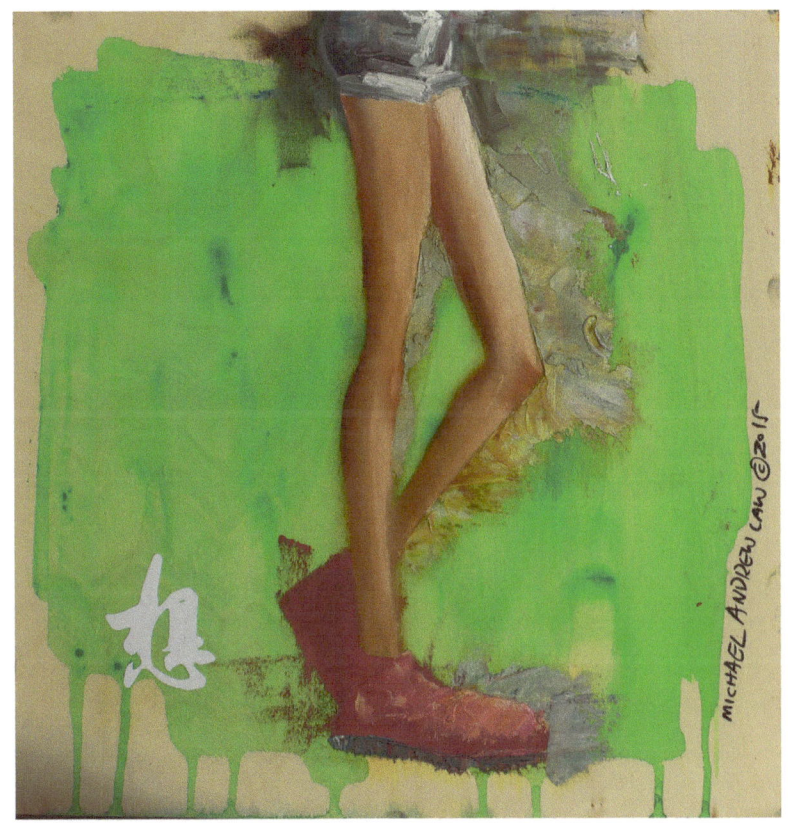

Oil , Glitter and Gold leaf on wood

12 x 12 inches

Private Collection

Michael Andrew Law

(852) 6444-7550

info@michaelandrewlaw.com

www.michaelandrewlaw.com

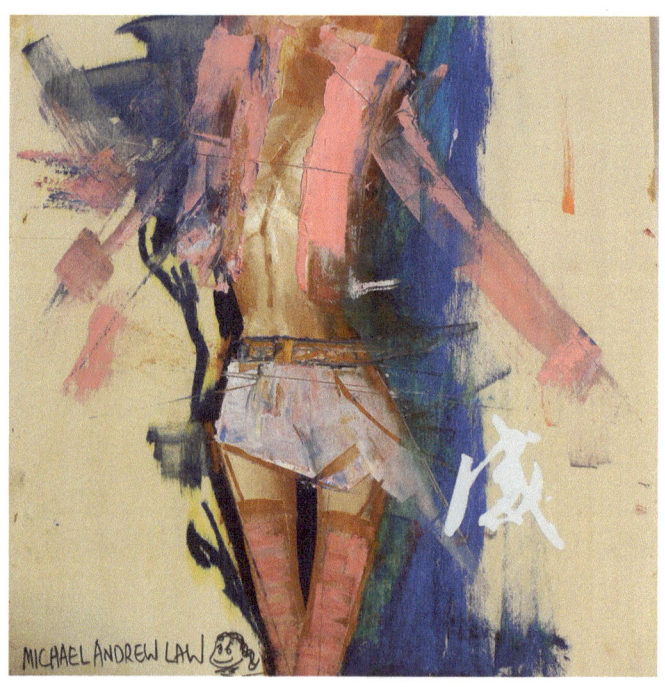

Oil , Glitter and Gold leaf on wood

12 x 12 inches

Private Collection

Michael Andrew Law

(852) 6444-7550
info@michaelandrewlaw.com
www.michaelandrewlaw.com

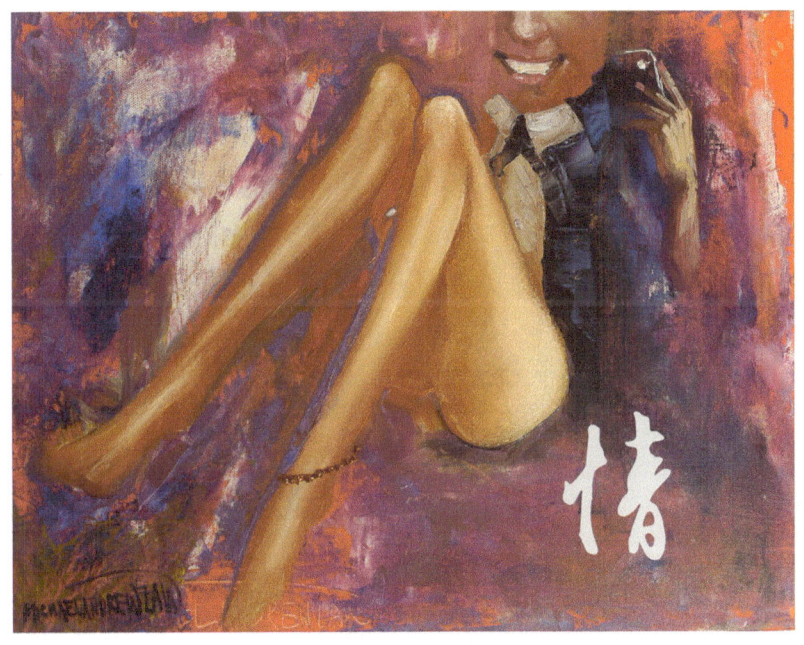

Oil , Glitter and Gold leaf on wood

12 x 12 inches

Private Collection

Michael Andrew Law

(852) 6444-7550

info@michaelandrewlaw.com

www.michaelandrewlaw.com

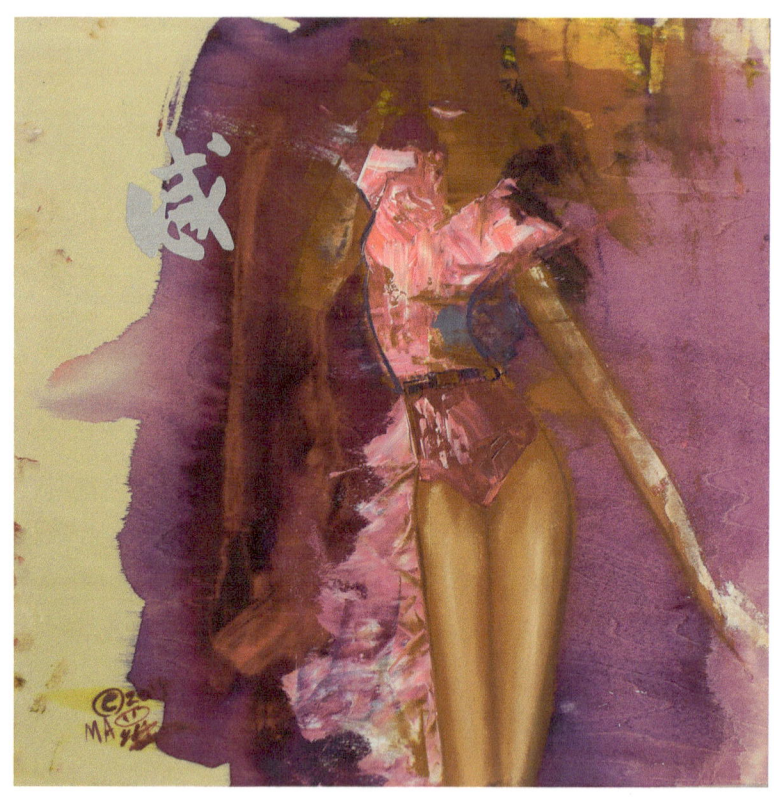

Oil , Glitter and Gold leaf on wood

12 x 12 inches

Private Collection

Michael Andrew Law
(852) 6444-7550
info@michaelandrewlaw.com
www.michaelandrewlaw.com

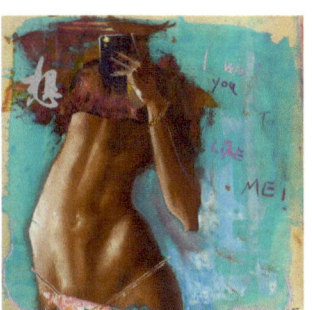

Oil , Glitter and Gold leaf on wood
12 x 12 inches
Private Collection

michaelandrewlaw_wood005

Michael Andrew Law
(852) 6444-7550
info@michaelandrewlaw.com
www.michaelandrewlaw.com

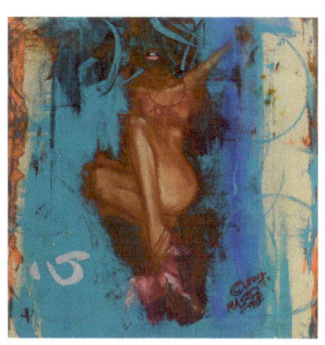

Oil , Glitter and Gold leaf on wood
12 x 12 inches
Private Collection

michaelandrewlaw_wood007

Michael Andrew Law
(852) 6444-7550
info@michaelandrewlaw.com
www.michaelandrewlaw.com

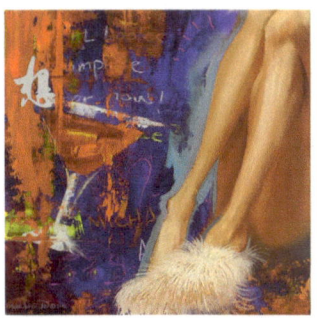

Oil , Glitter and Gold leaf on wood
12 x 12 inches
Private Collection

michaelandrewlaw_wood006

Michael Andrew Law
(852) 6444-7550
info@michaelandrewlaw.com
www.michaelandrewlaw.com

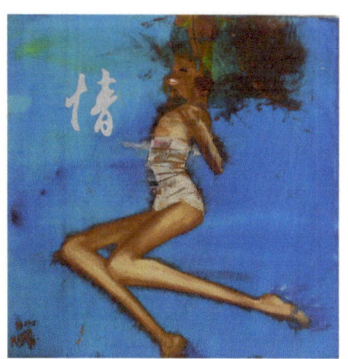

Oil , Glitter and Gold leaf on wood
12 x 12 inches
Private Collection

michaelandrewlaw_wood008

Michael Andrew Law
(852) 6444-7550
info@michaelandrewlaw.com
www.michaelandrewlaw.com

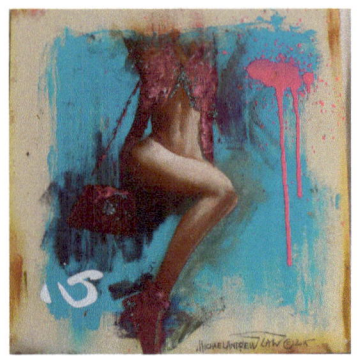

Oil , Glitter and Gold leaf on wood
12 x 12 inches
Private Collection

michaelandrewlaw_wood009

Michael Andrew Law
(852) 6444-7550
info@michaelandrewlaw.com
www.michaelandrewlaw.com

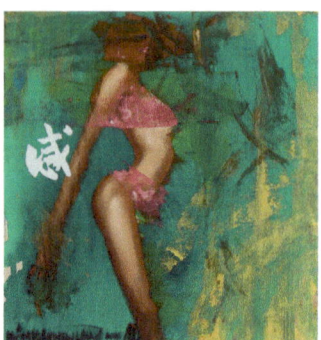

Oil , Glitter and Gold leaf on wood
12 x 12 inches
Private Collection

michaelandrewlaw_wood011

Michael Andrew Law
(852) 6444-7550
info@michaelandrewlaw.com
www.michaelandrewlaw.com

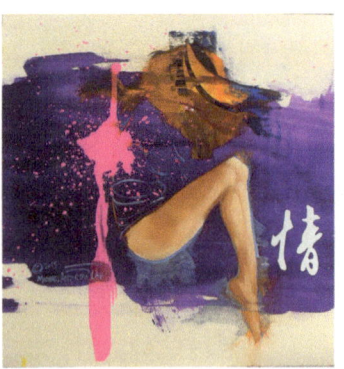

Oil , Glitter and Gold leaf on wood
12 x 12 inches
Private Collection

michaelandrewlaw_wood010

Michael Andrew Law
(852) 6444-7550
info@michaelandrewlaw.com
www.michaelandrewlaw.com

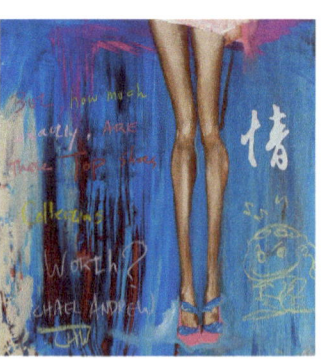

Oil , Glitter and Gold leaf on wood
12 x 12 inches
Private Collection

michaelandrewlaw_wood012

Michael Andrew Law
(852) 6444-7550
info@michaelandrewlaw.com
www.michaelandrewlaw.com

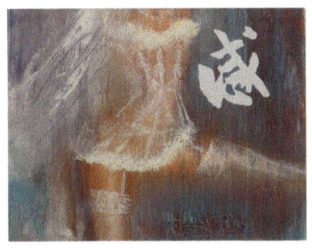

DETAILS of a painting
Oil , Glitter and Gold leaf on wood
12 x 12 inches
Private Collection

michaelandrewlaw_wood013

Michael Andrew Law
(852) 6444-7550
info@michaelandrewlaw.com
www.michaelandrewlaw.com

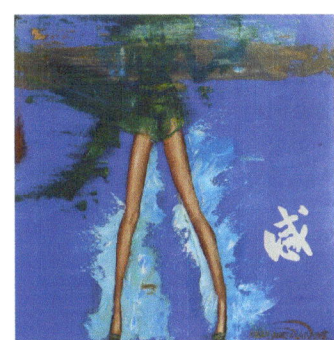

Oil , Glitter and Gold leaf on wood
12 x 12 inches
Private Collection

michaelandrewlaw_wood015

Michael Andrew Law
(852) 6444-7550
info@michaelandrewlaw.com
www.michaelandrewlaw.com

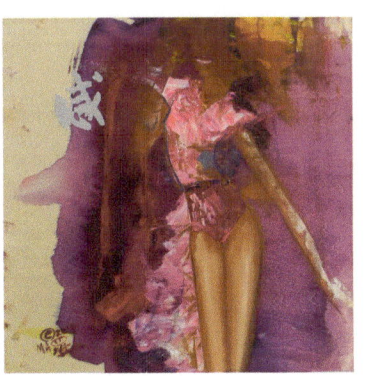

DETAILS of a painting
Oil , Glitter and Gold leaf on wood
12 x 12 inches
Private Collection

michaelandrewlaw_wood014

Michael Andrew Law
(852) 6444-7550
info@michaelandrewlaw.com
www.michaelandrewlaw.com

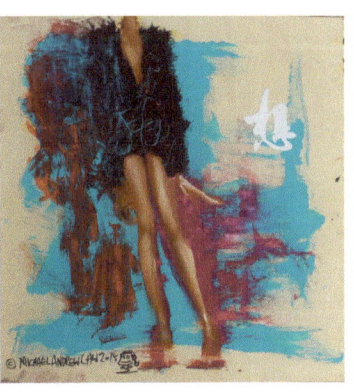

Oil , Glitter and Gold leaf on wood
12 x 12 inches
Private Collection

michaelandrewlaw_wood016

Michael Andrew Law
(852) 6444-7550
info@michaelandrewlaw.com
www.michaelandrewlaw.com

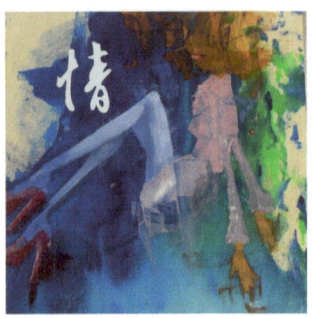

Oil , Glitter and Gold leaf on wood
12 x 12 inches
Private Collection

michaelandrewlaw_wood017

Michael Andrew Law
(852) 6444-7550
info@michaelandrewlaw.com
www.michaelandrewlaw.com

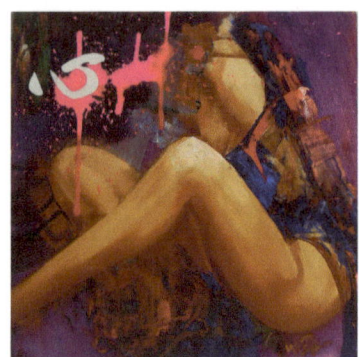

Oil , Glitter and Gold leaf on wood
12 x 12 inches
Private Collection

michaelandrewlaw_wood019

Michael Andrew Law
(852) 6444-7550
info@michaelandrewlaw.com
www.michaelandrewlaw.com

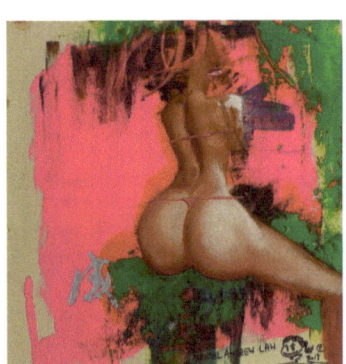

Oil , Glitter and Gold leaf on wood
12 x 12 inches
Private Collection

michaelandrewlaw_wood018

Michael Andrew Law
(852) 6444-7550
info@michaelandrewlaw.com
www.michaelandrewlaw.com

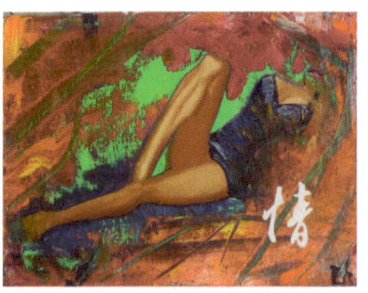

Oil , Glitter and Gold leaf on wood
12 x 12 inches
Private Collection

michaelandrewlaw_wood020

Michael Andrew Law
(852) 6444-7550
info@michaelandrewlaw.com
www.michaelandrewlaw.com

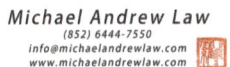

Michael Andrew Law
(852) 6444-7550
info@michaelandrewlaw.com
www.michaelandrewlaw.com

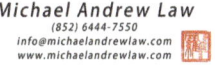

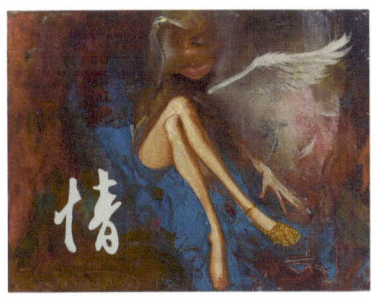

Oil , Glitter and Gold leaf on wood
12 x 12 inches
Private Collection

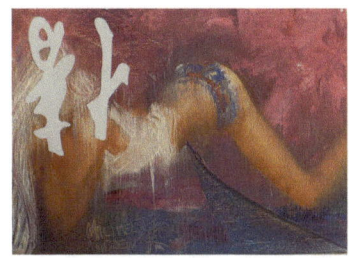

Oil , Glitter and Gold leaf on wood
12 x 12 inches
Private Collection

michaelandrewlaw_wood021

michaelandrewlaw_wood023

Michael Andrew Law
(852) 6444-7550
info@michaelandrewlaw.com
www.michaelandrewlaw.com

Michael Andrew Law
(852) 6444-7550
info@michaelandrewlaw.com
www.michaelandrewlaw.com

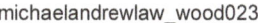

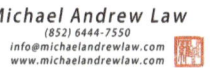

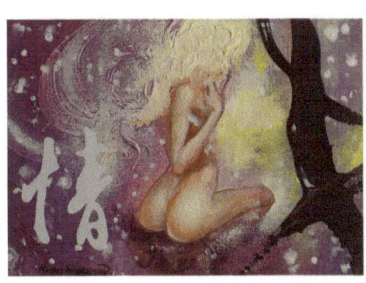

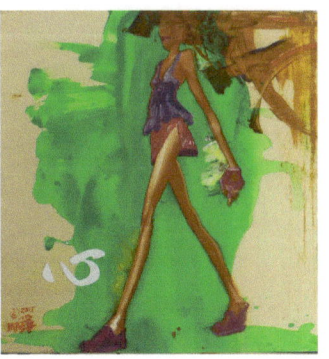

Oil , Glitter and Gold leaf on wood
12 x 12 inches
Private Collection

michaelandrewlaw_wood022

michaelandrewlaw_wood024

Michael Andrew Law
(852) 6444-7550
info@michaelandrewlaw.com
www.michaelandrewlaw.com

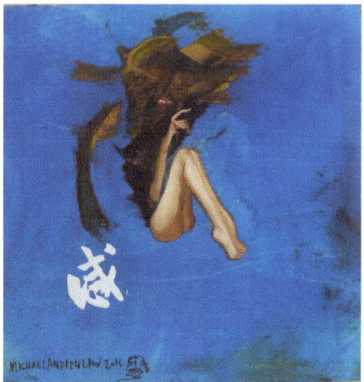

Oil , Glitter and Gold leaf on wood
12 x 12 inches
Private Collection

michaelandrewlaw_wood025

Michael Andrew Law
(852) 6444-7550
info@michaelandrewlaw.com
www.michaelandrewlaw.com

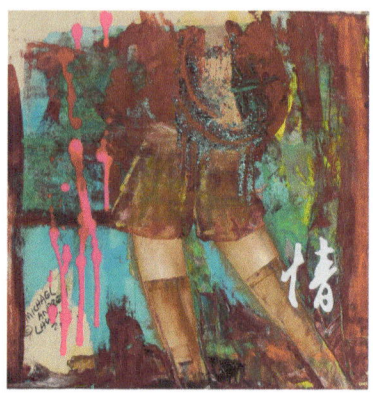

Oil , Glitter and Gold leaf on wood
12 x 12 inches
Private Collection

michaelandrewlaw_wood027

Michael Andrew Law
(852) 6444-7550
info@michaelandrewlaw.com
www.michaelandrewlaw.com

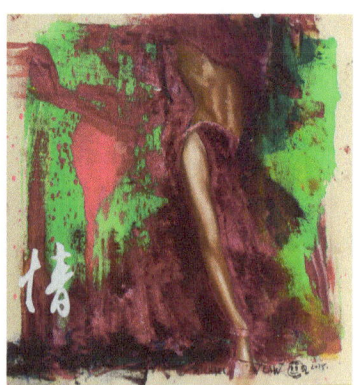

Oil , Glitter and Gold leaf on wood
12 x 12 inches
Private Collection

michaelandrewlaw_wood026

Michael Andrew Law
(852) 6444-7550
info@michaelandrewlaw.com
www.michaelandrewlaw.com

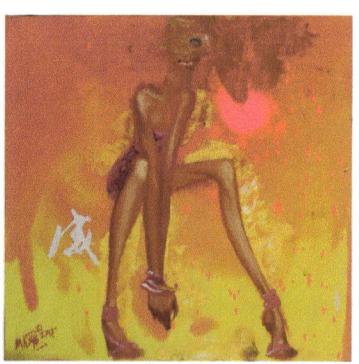

Oil , Glitter and Gold leaf on wood
12 x 12 inches
Private Collection

michaelandrewlaw_wood028

Michael Andrew Law
(852) 6444-7550
info@michaelandrewlaw.com
www.michaelandrewlaw.com

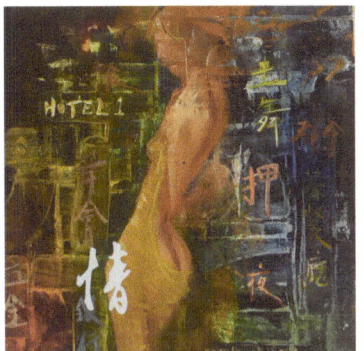

Oil , Glitter and Gold leaf on wood
12 x 12 inches
Private Collection

michaelandrewlaw_wood029

Michael Andrew Law
(852) 6444-7550
info@michaelandrewlaw.com
www.michaelandrewlaw.com

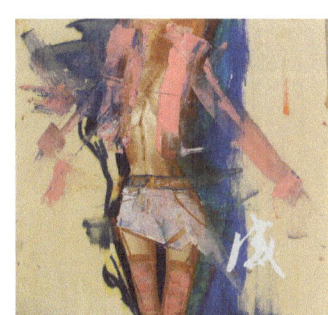

Oil , Glitter and Gold leaf on wood
12 x 12 inches
Private Collection

michaelandrewlaw_wood031

Michael Andrew Law
(852) 6444-7550
info@michaelandrewlaw.com
www.michaelandrewlaw.com

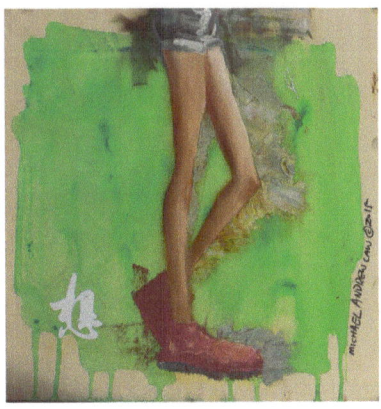

Oil , Glitter and Gold leaf on wood
12 x 12 inches
Private Collection

michaelandrewlaw_wood030

Michael Andrew Law
(852) 6444-7550
info@michaelandrewlaw.com
www.michaelandrewlaw.com

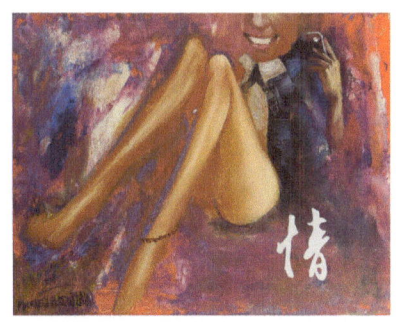

Oil , Glitter and Gold leaf on wood
12 x 12 inches
Private Collection

michaelandrewlaw_wood032

Michael Andrew Law
(852) 6444-7550
info@michaelandrewlaw.com
www.michaelandrewlaw.com

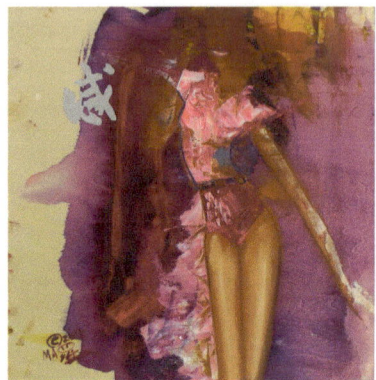

Oil , Glitter and Gold leaf on wood
12 x 12 inches
Private Collection

michaelandrewlaw_wood033

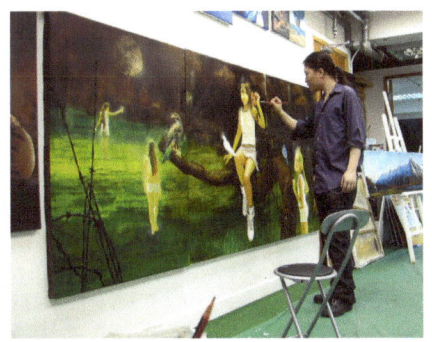

Michael Andrew Law at Work.

Michael Andrew Law fusing digital and classical painting with west and East creative philosophy , to produce an extremely original artistic language and content that bridged west and east ,classical and modern medium , at the same time clearly tells the stories of his own generation. Combining digital creative materials and classical painting techniques with effusive yet knowing and precise focused , his paintings maintain a powerful tension between opposing aesthetic forces—expression and knowledge, control and spontaneity, savagery and wit, urbanity and primitivism—while providing satiric commentary on the oppressive realities of the predicament of Generation Internet, homegrown hongkonger's local-culture vesus Traditional Chinese culture, and The Hong Kong's post-handover history.

In his dynamically designed compositions, gracefully detailed figures and innocent faces are incise against fields that juxtaposed with portraits, chinese calligraphy, and sometimes cgi. The Pale Hair Girls Series (2006 - 2013) depicts realistic cold, icy-like young female figures surrounded by abstract and expressively painted forms and shapes revealing images of Pop culture, Historial figures, and Hong Kong landmarks.

Michael Andrew Law draws inspiration from Old Master's works such as Caravaggio , Ruben , Rembrandt , all the way to the Modern Art Superstars such as Warhol , Lichtenstein , Richter , De Kooning , Bacon , Wool and Prince . The Pale Hair Girls series mainly inspired by the painting works of French academic painter and traditionalist William-Adolphe Bouguereau and the Late Great YiFei Chen's characteristic "Romantic Realism" paintings.

In a reversal of standard East-West aesthetics, Law re-interprets Old Master's sophisticated imagery combine classical and digital materials—which resonate with Digital Vector Designs and Paintings—with fine strokes of oil paint multi-layered with paint film.In his interpretation of Leonardo Da Vinci's iconic Mona Lisa's smile (1517)—an iconic image that has been endlessly disseminated and reproduced—Law painted over the symbolism of the portrait Mona Lisa with his young wife , intent on rendering the figure in contemporary fashion with the iconic image as background .

"The Humanity triptych" depicts New Generation HongKongers in a Ruined Hong Kong city , awaiting their unknown fate of a new beginning. This painting series explores one of the central paradox of his art—between romance and derision , his romantic magnanimity as an artist and his pessimistic perspective on the predicament of Generation Y Hongkongers. Here, this paradox is symbolized by the stark contrast of icy cold young female and disturbing representations of the armageddon-like of images. Whether portrayed as single "chinese calligraphy " or in triptych composition and classical paintwork that combine both expressive and traditional painting techniques with the digital vector , the beauties and the human figures stand as eternal motifs in the history of art and also in popular culture. Both oppositional and parallel, they are reminders of the fragile vibrancy of life and the impitoyable passing of time.

A references between different cultural refrence (high/pop, classical/contemporary, east/west), Michael Andrew Law has stated that an artist should be someone who understood how to hybrid between different worlds and go ahead makes an effort to knowing them. With his distinctive "iEgoism" philosophy , which employs highly refined academic painting techniques to depict a mixture of abstract expressionism within a representational pop culture images. These techniques parallel to the themes of romance and predicament of this generation , he recollects and revitalizes narratives of irony and introspection.

Michael Andrew Law was born in 1982 in British Hong Kong , studied fine art with american artist Daniel Anderson and with artist graduatee of China Central Academy of Fine Arts Sam Zeng from 2003 - 2006 . He co-founded the Hong Kong Art Studio Nature Art Workshop in 2008. In addition to the production and marketing of Michael Andrew Law's art and related work, Nature Art functions as a supportive environment for the
fostering of emerging Hong Konger artists. Law is also a curator. In 2013, he organized an exhibition of contemporary art titled "iEgoism ," which served as a commentaries of contemporary HongKong Gen Y pop culture ;These Theroy also published in the book : "iEgoism" in 2014.

Michael Andrew Law currently works and lives in Hong Kong.

For further information please contact the studio at info@michaelandrewlaw.com or at +852.6444.7550. All images are subject to copyright. Artist/Studio/Gallery's approval must be granted prior to reproduction.

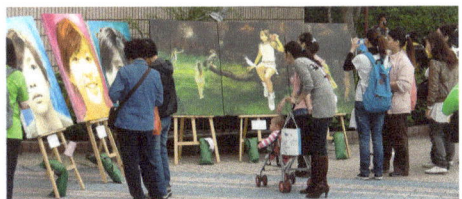

2010 Avenue of Stars, Hong Kong

Exhibition :

2013 DeTour Matters 2013 Satellite Events at NatureArt Gallery
2013 December to Remember , One man show at NatureArt Gallery Central District, Hong Kong.
2012 Solo Show , Park Central tseung kwan O ,Hong Kong
2011 Art Walk Group Showing , Discovery Bay ,Hong Kong
2011 HK Gold Coast (Book signing exhibition)
2009 Solo Painting Exhibition The Avenue of Stars
Group Exhibition of Daniel Anderson workshop Classical Realism class of 2008 at Manhattan,NY
2007 Guest and Exhibition The Peak Galleria Hong Kong
2007 Invited workshop exhibition, Elements, Hong Kong
Group Exhibition of Classical Realism class of 2007 at Manhattan,NY
2006 Collection by Cardinal Zen Ze-kiun and exhibited at Catholic Church of Hong Kong.
2004 - 2007, Hong Kong Young Artist Group Exhibition, Hong Kong Central Library.
Group Exhibition of Classical Realism class of 2006 at East Village, Manhattan,NY
2005 Illustration original exhibition for Kung Kao Po
2004 Group Exhibition, Wanchai Tower
2003 Group Exhibition, Hong Kong Convention and Exhibition Centre.
2003 Winner of I luv Hong Kong Painting Competition, exhibition at The Landmark (Hong Kong).
2002 The Holy story Picture Book illustrated picture original exhibition ,sai wan ho civic centre.

SELECTED COLLECTIONS :

Cardinal of the Catholic Church Joseph Zen Ze-kiun
Organic Beauty inc
Agriculture, Fisheries and Conservation Department
Ms.Ho Wei Ying
Ms. Annie Yu
Daniel Anderson
MR.Tsang Yan Sam   /

PUBLICATIONS :

Fisheye magazine , featured artist interview , November 2002
Kung Kao Po , interview , June 2006
Art of Rock Realism , 2008
The Art of Michael Andrew Law , 2010
December to Remember One man Show Art Book , 2013
iEgoism , 2015

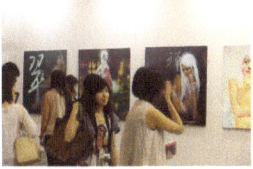

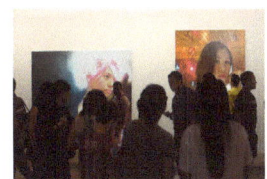

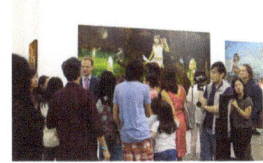

Solo Shows 2010 - 2013

Each limited edition print is proofed, signed and numbered by Michael Andrew Law personally.

Pigment prints are the newest generation of digital fine art printing with a very fine resolution and the highest light resistance, and are accepted by museums and galleries worldwide as the leading standard in art reproduction.

Order Limited Edition / Paintings :
Please contact us by email:
info@michaelandrewlaw.com to place your order, or for any other questions.

Disclaimer:

All sales are final once payment is made. All prints are safely packaged for shipping and are carefully reviewed for perfection before shipment, but should the prints be damaged by Fedex carriers somehow we will replace the damaged print at no extra cost.

Please also be aware that sizes given are approximate, that some details and colors of prints may differ slightly to what is seen over the web, but that all prints are thouroughly checked for quality and accuracy by the artist personally.

www.ingramcontent.com/pod-product-compliance
Lightning Source LLC
Chambersburg PA
CBHW040747200526
45159CB00023B/1768